tough topics

600 questions that will take your students beneath the surface

Jim Aitkins

■ ZONDERVAN®

ZONDERVAN.com/
AUTHORTRACKER
follow your favorite authors

Youth Specialties
.com

Youth Specialties

Tough Topics: 600 Questions That Will Take Take Your Students Beneath the Surface
Copyright © 2003 by Youth Specialties

Youth Specialties products, 300 South Pierce Street, El Cajon, CA 92020, are published by Zondervan, 5300 Patterson Aveune SE, Grand Rapids, MI 49530

Library of Congress Cataloging-in-Publication Data

ISBN-10: 0-310-24109-X
ISBN-13: 0-310-24109-6

Edited by Tamara Rice
Cover and interior design by Proxy

Printed in the United States of America

07 08 09 10 11 12 13 14 15 • 15 14 13 12 11 10 9 8 7 6 5

Dedication
To Hailey, my sweet daughter—a source of much joy and
many, many questions.

From the Author

Today's average teenager watches more hours of television, goes to more movies, and plays more video games than ever. Among other things, it's quite possible that this troubling trend is helping to create a nonanalytical, nonverbal, and non-believing generation.

But can one book turn things around? Absolutely.

Of course that book is the Bible.

As far as this book is concerned, though, its purpose is to arouse a renewed interest in Scripture as the ultimate source of wisdom and answers to life's most profound challenges. And maybe—just maybe—this collection of tough questions can help young people become better at analyzing things (like right and wrong) and verbalizing their thoughts. And after that, who knows—maybe lives could be changed.

We've all been told that you don't know unless you ask. Well, knowing is just one of the benefits of asking teenagers these questions. As you will soon see—if you don't already know—questions can be a powerful teaching tool. Questions can help spur a discussion or even a friendly debate, and a few well-placed questions can feed an otherwise starving relationship.

That's why this book—even though it's primarily geared toward getting your students thinking and processing—really isn't just for youth group leaders or students. It's for parents and families as well. Imagine a divorced dad sitting in a restaurant, wanting to connect with his 12-year-old daughter sitting across from him, but they don't get much time together—could the questions in this book break the ice and get conversation started? Any family hoping to get their kids talking will benefit from these questions—whether they're used around the dinner table, in the car, or even as part of a home-school routine. Questions aimed at getting students talking aren't just for youth groups anymore.

I'd love to get your feedback, even if you just have a question! Email me at jdaitkins@earthlink.net.

Because of Christ,
Jim Aitkins

Contents

Are You Ready to Dive Below the Surface?

Should crucial life choices be based on feelings—which are changeable—or on a solid foundation of thoughts informed by teachings and principles that are unchangeable?

In an effort to take your students beyond mere opinion and emotion, each question in this book begins with either "Which would be better?" or "Which would be worse?" This kind of wording typically requires a solid determination instead of just an emotional estimation.

You'll also notice the "Taking It Deeper" boxes in the first section—you can use them to offer commentary that'll get your students thinking more critically about specific topics. Feel free to read the commentary to your students word-for-word, or if you wish, alter the text to suit your tastes and your students' needs.

There are also "nonsense" questions to inject a little levity into the discussions—or to just throw your students completely off the path! Either way, it should be fun.

The last time I checked, there was no peer pressure—among any age group—to either sleep in an itchy wool suit or a bed of fiberglass insulation. But asking students to express definitive judgments on harmless topics is a great way to get them to take risks and speak their minds. Taking stands on the things that really matter is a learned skill; it doesn't come naturally. Starting small with subjects that are risk-free, inane, quirky, and silly can be a fun way to begin that all-important learning process.

Now take the plunge!

275

Questions on Tough Topics about Life, Relationships, and God

1. Which would be *better?*

Working through a difficult problem on your own or having someone give you the answer

2. Which would be *worse?*

Performing mouth-to-mouth resuscitation on an alcoholic bum or having someone sneeze in your face

3. Which would be *better?*

Playing video games or shopping with birthday money

4. Which would be *worse?*

Looking for water in the desert or making a fire in the snowy Arctic Circle

5. Which would be *better?*

Being head custodian at the White House or president of the United States

6. Which would be *worse?*

Losing the Super Bowl or having a losing season

7. Which would be *better?*

Being gifted at remembering names
or remembering information

8. Which would be *better?*

Being a preacher or a popular Las
Vegas entertainer

Taking It Deeper
[A Thought to Consider]

Everyone wants to be popular, and most people desire to
be wealthy, but very few people would choose a job that
includes being unpopular at times and not being very
wealthy, ever. How would you answer if the last question if
it were rephrased: "Which would be better—being rich and
striving for popularity or being poor and pursuing God's
will in your life?"

---

9. Which would be *worse?*

Being tongue-tied in front of a large
audience or vomiting on yourself on
an airplane

10. Which would be *worse?*

Never eating pizza again or never
wearing stylish clothing again

11. **Which would be _better?_**

Owning the world's largest collection of hubcaps or 8-track tapes

12. **Which would be _worse?_**

Getting stuck with the heifer leg of a coffee table on the elevator or being jarred loose from a strawberry jelly nuance

13. **Which would be _worse?_**

Having a heart attack or losing a limb

14. **Which would be _worse?_**

Rejecting someone or being rejected by someone

Taking It Deeper
[A Thought to Consider]

Jesus never condemned anyone who came to him for mercy and forgiveness, but he was ultimately rejected and killed by those he came to accept and forgive. If we want to follow Jesus' example, we should be unwilling to reject anyone—but totally willing to be rejected for his sake. Because Jesus was rejected, the entire world has been forever blessed.

---

15. **Which would be** *better?*

Eating granola or oatmeal

16. **Which would be** *better?*

Being a highly paid singer or a professional athlete

17. **Which would be** *better?*

Asking questions or giving answers

18. **Which would be** *worse?*

Having no voice or suffering excruciating pain for the rest of your life

19. **Which would be** *better?*

Leaving a large inheritance or spending all your wealth before you die

20. **Which would be** *worse?*

Never being able to laugh or never being able to cry

21. **Which would be** *better?*

Going to a private Christian school or a public school

22. Which would be *worse?*

Losing your memory or losing your friends

23. Which would be *better?*

Being a good cook or good artist

24. Which would be *worse?*

Being ridiculed on national television or winning an award that should have gone to someone else

---

Taking It Deeper
[A Thought to Consider]

The world says, "Make yourself look good at all costs." So according to the world, if you live the Bible's advice to seek the good of others and put the interests of others before your own (1 Corinthians 10:24; 13:5 and Philippians 2:4), you are being a fool. But guess what? The Bible says, "We are fools for Christ" (1 Corinthians 4:10). In other words, if you're a follower of Jesus, that means you may be mocked and ridiculed for doing what he commands.

---

25. Which would be *better?*

Failing to climb Mt. Everest or successfully climbing a much smaller peak

26. **Which would be** *worse?*

Having a terminal illness or being in a coma for 30 years before waking up

27. **Which would be** *worse?*

Being stuck alone on an island for 10 years or enduring a yearlong road trip in the back seat of a hot, crowded van

28. **Which would be** *better?*

Paying less for last year's hot clothing item or paying more for something trendy now

---

Taking It Deeper
[A Thought to Consider]

God wants you to be a good steward with money. The fact is any money you have actually belongs to God; he's just seen fit to let you use it. If God were testing you on how wisely you spend his money, would you pass the test?

---

29. **Which would be** *worse?*

Wearing braces on your teeth for 10 years or on your legs for one year

30. Which would be *better?*

Being considered rude but generous or smelly but loyal

31. Which would be *worse?*

Taking an ice-cold shower or bathing in a warm—but dirty—pond

32. Which would be *better?*

Helping an elderly woman cross the street or helping friends do their homework

33. Which would be *worse?*

Fumbling the basketball just before you were about to score a goal or being the losing coach of a havarti team

34. Which would be *better?*

Listening to a riveting story on the radio or watching a lame story on television

35. Which would be *worse?*

Someone regularly biting your nails for you or clipping them yourself only once a year

36. **Which would be *better?***

Receiving a high school diploma after only one year of classes or receiving it with honors after attending an extra year of school and graduating a year later than your friends

37. **Which would be *worse?***

Getting caught picking your nose on national television or having your pants fall down on national television

38. **Which would be *worse?***

Never getting a joke or always saying things others don't understand

---

Taking It Deeper
[A Thought to Consider]

Sometimes it's easier to wander through a whole conundrum of fortuitous, meandering quandaries—causing mental depictions of peculiar notions (not necessarily aiming at one objective discernable to the average person, yet still bringing forth the circumstances under which a mystifying gathering of cerebral interactions not normally taking place cause an abnormally high level of mirth) where people are both amused and confounded—than to keep things at their typically and predictably comprehensible state of status quo.

39. **Which would be *better*?**
Playing baseball or football

40. **Which would be *worse*?**
Taking a pop quiz or being laughed at because you accidentally splashed water on the front of your pants while washing your hands

41. **Which would be *better*?**
Having a high-paying but unchallenging, boring job or an average-paying but fun, challenging job

42. **Which would be *worse*?**
Spending a night alone, outside, during a thunderstorm or spending a night alone inside a creepy, old house

43. **Which would be *worse*?**
Getting caught cheating on a test or being forced to tell on a cheating friend

44. **Which would be *better*?**
Seeing a movie at the theater or waiting until the movie comes out on video

45. **Which would be *better*?**

Being the ruler of a nation where
most citizens claim to love God but
don't love their neighbors or the
ruler of a nation where most citizens
claim to be atheists but are generally
good, moral people

Taking It Deeper
[A Thought to Consider]

Neither place exists or has ever existed—not even during
biblical times. That may sound like a pretty black-and-white
statement, but it's absolutely true. So powerful is the influence of Jesus that when and where he is not honored and
served, his absence is noticed. The opposite is also true—
when and where he's loved and served, his presence is
tangible.

---

46. **Which would be *worse*?**

Eating only cottage cheese for a
year or being responsible for all the
housework as long as you live in
your parents' house

47. **Which would be *better*?**

Walking a mile on level ground or a
mile over hills and through valleys

48. **Which would be *worse*?**

Losing a limb or badly burning your face

Taking It Deeper
[A Thought to Consider]

We live in a time when looking good means more than just about anything else. When we say it would be worse to badly burn our faces or lose our limbs, what are we really saying? Next time you're in public and see someone who looks…well…different from you, resist the natural impulse to stare. Ask yourself what Jesus would do, and do it the first chance you get.

---

49. **Which would be *worse*?**

Striking out in the last game of the World Series or getting hit in the elbow in the last game of the World Series

50. **Which would be *worse*?**

Getting hit by lightning or by a car

51. **Which would be *worse*?**

Giving up walking or laughing

52. Which would be *better?*

Vacationing for two weeks to an exciting place you've never been (with hardly any money) or skipping your vacation to work for two weeks for triple your pay

53. Which would be *better?*

Working for a large company or working for yourself

54. Which would be *better?*

Playing a game of football with no referees or playing it with unfair referees

55. Which would be *better?*

Being the only person with a lifetime supply of ball-peen hammer ice cream or being able to share a small amount of contra-indicated Turkish delights with your friends only once

56. Which would be *worse?*

Not being able to read or not being able to smell

57. Which would be *better?*

Eating cookies or drinking milk

58. Which would be *better?*

Showing up at the prom in a brand-new Mercedes limousine while you (or your date) are wearing a powder blue '70s tuxedo or showing up in a beat-up '82 Chevy Vega wearing the best-looking tux in the place

59. Which would be *worse?*

Having no date for the prom or having a group date of friends for the prom

60. Which would be *better?*

Going to the prom with the most popular person or the most honorable person

61. Which would be *worse?*

Getting stuck in traffic and missing half the prom or making it to the prom on time but with a huge ketchup stain on the front of your gown or tux the entire evening

62. Which would be *better?*

Leaving the prom with the most popular person in school (who you suspect may want to have sex with you before the evening ends) or leaving the prom alone or with friends (when you know you'll get laughed at the next day)?

Taking It Deeper
[A Thought to Consider]

Every school year countless Christian students find themselves in situations like this. But the most important thing to remember is that you're responsible for the decisions you make—God isn't (see James 1:13-15). In the Lord's Prayer we say, "Lead us not into temptation" (Matthew 6:13). So stay as far from temptation as you can (Proverbs 1:10), and God will give you the strength to resist (1 Corinthians 10:13 and Hebrews 2:18).

63. Which would be *worse?*

Standing for eight hours or sleeping for eight hours on someone else's dirty sheets

64. Which would be *better?*

Doing housework or yard work

65. Which would be *worse?*

Driving through an area recently sprayed by a skunk or driving past a large dairy farm

66. Which would be *better?*

Owning a house made of brick or a house with wood siding

67. Which would be *worse?*

Being known as a selfish tightwad or as a hypocrite

Taking It Deeper
[A Thought to Consider]

Some people who don't give money to homeless people are considered selfish or stingy—even when their reasons are (usually) that they don't want them spending money on alcohol or drugs. So which would be worse—giving money to an alcoholic homeless person or being considered a hypocrite saying you love your neighbor but not putting that love into action?

---

68. Which would be *better?*

Frolicking in a cave hideout or a tree house

69. Which would be *worse?*

Getting shot in the foot with a gun or in the rear end with an arrow

70. Which would be *better?*

Traveling in a time machine to the past or to the future

71. Which would be *worse?*

Sitting through a three-hour church business meeting or flunking a subject in school and taking it over again

72. Which would be *better?*

Having courage or wisdom

Taking It Deeper
[A Thought to Consider]

Which of the two—courage or wisdom—is more likely to help you in a time of trouble? Which of the two would be more likely to keep you out of trouble in the first place?

---

73. Which would be *worse?*

Mowing the grass at a cemetery or sweeping the floors of a nursing home

74. Which would be *better?*

Eating a sundae or drinking a shake

75. Which would be *worse?*

Hearing a gut-wrenching scream while taking a walk in the woods or being awakened by strange footsteps in your house in the middle of the night

76. Which would be *better?*

Sitting in a hot tub or getting a massage

77. Which would be *worse?*

Being Adam or Eve when faced with the serpent

Taking It Deeper
[A Thought to Consider]

Adam received God's instruction and was responsible for sharing it with Eve—he must not have done a very good job. And instead of reiterating what God told him when they were tempted by the serpent, Adam remained silent. (See Genesis 3.)

78. **Which would be** *better?*

Living in a nice house on a street lined with big, beautiful trees or living in a nice house at the top of a bare hill with a great view

79. **Which would be** *worse?*

Having a day where everything goes wrong or having a completely sleepless night

80. **Which would be** *better?*

Getting to choose your entrée or your dessert

81. **Which would be** *worse?*

Being questioned as a terrorist then released or being seriously injured by a terrorist attack

82. **Which would be** *worse?*

Having five teeth drilled for cavities or memorizing a chapter of Leviticus

83. **Which would be** *better?*

Being valued for your wisdom or your generosity

Taking It Deeper
[A Thought to Consider]

Any time you can share wisdom with another person, you are being generous. Give away a valuable piece of insight, and you'll benefit someone many times over. Give someone a dollar out of the generosity of your heart and tomorrow—as long as she lacks wisdom—she may need another dollar tomorrow. Of course this is no excuse for not helping others financially or materially—you should be generous! Just be wise in your generosity.

84. **Which would be *better*?**

Going bankrupt after being a millionaire or going bankrupt after owning very little

85. **Which would be *worse*?**

Witnessing an execution or a fatal car accident

86. **Which would be *better*?**

Buying a car or leasing one

87. **Which would be *worse*?**

Being really jittery from drinking too much coffee or being forced to drink a quart of buttermilk

88. Which would be *better?*

Drinking ice-cold water or ice-cold Gatorade

89. Which would be *better?*

Being the villager of an executive club of pea farmers or being able to achieve whirled peas

90. Which would be *better?*

Winning a pillow fight or water fight

91. Which would be *worse?*

Three large canker sores in your mouth or a very congested nose

92. Which would be *worse?*

Three friends tickling you or sitting on you

93. Which would be *better?*

Swimming or snow skiing

94. Which would be *worse?*

Coughing with a sore throat or walking on a sore ankle

95. Which would be *better?*

Water skiing or roller-blading

96. Which would be *worse?*

Being mistaken for a purse snatcher and beaten up by a mob or being fired by your boss because you refused to lie to a customer

Taking It Deeper
[A Thought to Consider]

If you were beaten up, at least you'd still have your job—that is, unless your boss was one of the people in the mob! And if you were mistakenly beaten up or unjustly fired, at least you'd have your integrity.

97. Which would be *worse?*

Being a prisoner of war or a hostage in a bank holdup

98. Which would be *worse?*

Being held up for 15 minutes at a railroad crossing or being the last in a line of 20 people at the grocery store

99. Which would be *better?*

Being good at playing the drums or the trumpet

100. Which would be *better?*

Playing pool or foosball

101. Which would be *worse?*

Changing a baby's dirty diaper or a baby throwing up on you

102. Which would be *better?*

Receiving an unexpected apology or an unexpected discount on a purchase

Taking It Deeper
[A Thought to Consider]

Sales come along all the time. Apologies are so rare—we should treasure them. Look around—people are often rude, and many are too proud to apologize for their rudeness. So when someone does apologize, receive it! It will only be a matter of time before you may have to make an apology, too.

103. Which would be *better?*

Going back five years in your life with the knowledge you have now or forward five years with the knowledge you have now

104. Which would be *worse?*

Never being able to retire or never being able to find a job

105. Which would be *better?*

Going on the vacation of your dreams or owning the car of your dreams but never traveling as long as you own it

106. Which would be *better?*

Eating mashed potatoes with gravy or with a thick, juicy steak

107. Which would be *worse?*

Being stranded alone on a cliff or on a raft in the middle of the ocean

108. Which would be *better?*

Camping in a tent or in an RV

109. Which would be *worse?*

Walking on hot coals or on a bed of nails

110. Which would be *better?*

Writing an action-packed, best-selling book about the travels of a magnificent seafaring vessel or living the actual experience as captain of the ship

---

Taking It Deeper
[A Thought to Consider]

If you write a book without living the experience, you'll just be writing things that others have said and written and done. As the captain, you would be able to live the experience. Why not be a captain for a while...then come ashore and write a book about it! Some people might say, "I hate ships. I'd get seasick!" Well, if you were the captain of a ship, you'd would be able to write books about sailing *and* barfing—what could be better?

---

111. Which would be *better?*

The possibility of great wealth (but with the risk of lifelong poverty, too) or the assurance you'll always have just what you need (but no more)

112. **Which would be *worse?***

Sleeping in an itchy wool suit or a bed of fiberglass insulation

113. **Which would be *worse?***

Fixing septic tanks or being a telemarketer

114. **Which would be *better?***

Being free from worry or always having joy

115. **Which would be *worse?***

Having no sense of humor or no common sense

Taking It Deeper
[A Thought to Consider]

Some people laugh their way from one blithering blunder to the next. On the other hand, some very logical people don't know when to relax and have a good time. But is it really worse to lack common sense than to not know when to laugh? Isn't it possible to be happy without always catching the meaning of a joke?

116. **Which would be *better?***

Having incredible strength or incredible intelligence

117. **Which would be *worse?***

Going to prison for one year for driving drunk and injuring someone or going to prison for five years for something you didn't do

118. **Which would be *better?***

Going on the Internet with severance codes that make your connection more dilapidated or using an E-series micron spectrometer while driving on the freeway

119. **Which would be *worse?***

Being too hot or too cold

120. **Which would be *better?***

Having enough time to do whatever you want or enough money to do whatever you want

121. Which would be *worse?*

Eating a bowl of granola without milk or chewing a piece of aluminum foil

122. Which would be *better?*

Playing miniature golf or bowling

123. Which would be *worse?*

Becoming a parent out of wedlock or being wrongly convicted of murder

124. Which would be *worse?*

Being alone all the time or lying to hold on to your friends

Taking It Deeper
[A Thought to Consider]

It's sad but true that some people lie just to have friends. Remember that God's promise to Joshua is a promise to us today. God will never leave us if we're trying to walk obediently in his steps (Joshua 1:7-9). If you lie just to have friends, eventually those friends will see you for the phony you are, and they'll leave. Then where will you be, after wandering from God and chasing your friends away?

125. Which would be *better?*

Having a hot drink on a cold day or a cold drink on a hot day

126. Which would be *better?*

Having five minutes to make an important decision with many expert advisors to help you or having 24 hours to make the same decision by yourself

127. Which would be *worse?*

Getting a speeding ticket or a really bad haircut

128. Which would be *better?*

Selling real estate or cars

129. Which would be *worse?*

Waxing and polishing a car or thoroughly vacuuming it out

130. Which would be *better?*

Praying for a friend for five minutes or talking to a friend about his problems for an hour

Taking It Deeper

[A Thought to Consider]

The Bible says we should share things with each other and confess things to each other. But it also says, "The prayer of a righteous man is powerful and effective" (James 5:16). Talking to each other and holding each other accountable is important, but there is real power in prayer. Even a five-minute prayer can change things like nothing else can—it could even change you!

131. Which would be *better?*

Buying everything you need at a garage sale or a thrift store

132. Which would be *worse?*

Having the batteries in your Walkman die during a long car trip or having a brand new Walkman break right after you buy it

133. Which would be *better?*

Meeting Abraham Lincoln or Martin Luther King, Jr.

134. Which would be *worse?*

Having one serious disappointment after another in your life or never being able to trust anyone

Taking It Deeper
[A Thought to Consider]

Some people have trouble trusting anyone because their trust has been violated one too many times in the past. It's just too great a risk to trust anyone again, and hurting people sometimes feel that way toward God. But Psalm 23—one of the most famous Bible passages—says God is with us and provides for us through hard times. God can always be trusted, even when others cannot be trusted.

135. Which would be *worse?*
Having an obnoxious ingrown hair or a particularly pesky sliver in the bottom of your foot

136. Which would be *better?*
Being paid to play your favorite sport or being paid to eat your favorite food

137. Which would be *worse?*
Hiking three hours into a three-day hike before realizing you forgot to bring food or running out of gas on a remote road

138. Which would be *worse?*
Being an impatient person or an inconsiderate person

139. *Which would be* ***better?***

Meeting an important person from anytime in history or getting to learn all about your future spouse before you actually meet

140. *Which would be* ***worse?***

A family member getting killed by a terrorist or a family member suddenly dying from an unknown illness

141. *Which would be* ***better?***

Living during the Civil War or the Revolutionary War

142. *Which would be* ***better?***

Asking a perfect stranger to loan you 20 bucks or swiping it from a stingy friend who'll never miss it

143. *Which would be* ***better?***

Working with wood or working with clay

144. *Which would be* ***worse?***

Going to the grand opening of a library or a modern art museum

145. Which would be *worse?*
Learning everything there is to know about construction or all there is to know about lethargistics

146. Which would be *better?*
Eating something sweet and buttery or salty and juicy

147. Which would be *better?*
Spending the night in a space station high above the earth or spending a cloudless, peaceful night just a few minutes from the summit of Mt. Everest

148. Which would be *better?*
A walk on the beach or in the forest

149. Which would be *worse?*
Slipping and injuring yourself in the bathtub (unable to reach anything but a phone to call the paramedics to your aid) or accidentally driving over a cliff in the mountains (but walking away without a scratch)

150. Which would be *worse?*

Finding yourself in a foreign land unable to speak the language or finding yourself alone outdoors and suddenly unable to see

151. Which would be *better?*

Being a rich contributor to a charitable cause or a person of modest means who spends time with a fatherless grade-school kid

Taking It Deeper
[A Thought to Consider]

Of course most people will say that it would be better to spend time with the fatherless grade-school kid, but how many people would really be willing to do that? When it comes right down to it, wouldn't more people rather be rich, enjoying that exciting lifestyle and getting praise for being so generous? Where is the fun and glory in merely spending time with a kid no one knows or cares about?

Giving a monetary gift may provide momentary glory and satisfaction (and certainly a lot of help to the charity), but the reward of a special relationship with someone who needs you is a pleasure that can last a lifetime.

152. **Which would be *better*?**

Being the judge on a murder trial or one of the jurors

153. **Which would be *worse*?**

Coughing up phlegm in public or blood at home

154. **Which would be *worse*?**

Drinking a glass of lukewarm milk that sat out all night or drinking a glass of cool water that was recently a bug's watery grave

155. **Which would be *better*?**

Knowing the entire Bible by heart or spending a week with Jesus in the flesh

156. **Which would be *better*?**

Going whale-watching or seeing a volcano erupt

157. **Which would be *better*?**

Eating a cheeseburger or veggie burger

158. Which would be *better?*

Making a lot of mistakes as a committed follower of Christ or making very few mistakes as an unbeliever

---

Taking It Deeper
[A Thought to Consider]

Sometimes very sincere people chose not to put their faith in Christ because they think they have to be "good" before God will accept them. This just isn't so. The Bible says, "While we were still sinners Christ died for us"(Romans 5:8). And Romans 3:23 says, "All have sinned and fall short of the glory of God." Both Christians and non-Christians will always make mistakes, but only those who choose to put their faith in Christ and receive him as Savior can be saved from their sin. So which would be better—being severely punished for one mistake or completely forgiven for many?

---

159. Which would be *better?*

Receiving a generous allowance for doing most of the household chores or having no housework responsibilities and no allowance

160. Which would be *worse?*

Dropping the three-tiered cake at a wedding or spilling all the soup at a shelter for the homeless

161. **Which would be *worse?***

Falling off a cliff or being run over by a steamroller

162. **Which would be *better?***

Having parents who are like best friends to you or parents who are more like caring teachers

163. **Which would be *worse?***

Not knowing if your parents really love you or knowing that as a baby you were abandoned by parents who didn't care

Taking It Deeper
[A Thought to Consider]

God does give our earthly parents the responsibility to raise us lovingly and in his wisdom, but let's face it—they aren't perfect. The Bible itself is full of examples of imperfect parents, like Adam, Jacob, and King David—just to name a few. But God's Word is reassuring to anyone who's ever been disappointed—or even betrayed—by parents. The Bible tells us God is our true father and tells how caring he is, how much he loves us, and how he's willing to guide our steps when we follow him in faith. Think of how wonderful it will be when the disappointments and betrayals of this world are finally over. Revelation 21:4 says, "There will be no more death or mourning or crying or pain" and God "will wipe every tear from [our] eyes"—now that's a father!

164. *Which would be worse?*

Getting kicked in the shins or slapped in the face

165. *Which would be better?*

Giving $240 to an outreach ministry or personally sponsoring a child overseas for $20 a month

166. *Which would be worse?*

Being annoyed by a mosquito or irritated by someone who talks too much

167. *Which would be better?*

Celebrating your birthday with no presents or celebrating Christmas with no presents

168. *Which would be worse?*

People always forgetting your name or your best friend betraying you

169. *Which would be better?*

Being the king of a walled city long ago or the mayor of a large city today

170. **Which would be *worse?***

Being punished for killing someone in self-defense or living with the guilt of accidentally causing someone's death

---

Taking It Deeper
[A Thought to Consider]

Whenever people die in accidents, often those who caused the accidents live with guilt for the rest of their lives. People die every day, and we live with that fact and merrily go on with our lives—but if someone's death were your fault, you probably wouldn't live with that so well. Why do you suppose that is?

---

171. **Which would be *better?***

Taking a cross-country train ride or a one-week trip to Disneyland

172. **Which would be *worse?***

Sleeping with no pillow or no blanket

173. **Which would be *better?***

Having a terminal illness and the support of many friends or having perfect health but no friends

Taking It Deeper

[A Thought to Consider]

Some people believe that if you have your health, you have everything. Others believe that a life without friends isn't worth living. The reality is that neither situation would be very desirable, but both situations would be easier if you had Jesus as your support on earth and your welcoming father in heaven.

174. Which would be *worse?*

No longer being able to play an instrument you once played extremely well or never being able to travel beyond a three-mile radius of home

175. Which would be *better?*

Going skydiving or attending the Super Bowl

176. Which would be *worse?*

Losing all the family photo albums in a fire or losing all the valuable family heirlooms

177. Which would be *worse?*

Living in a house with no windows or in a house made entirely of windows—with no window coverings

178. Which would be *better?*

Helping one person personally or many people anonymously

179. Which would be *worse?*

Winning a million-dollar lottery but having to use the money for a million-dollar surgery or never winning the lottery but enjoying good health

---

Taking It Deeper
[A Thought to Consider]

Check out Proverbs 28:19-20, Luke 12:15, 1 Timothy 6:9, and Hebrews 13:5. All of these verses discourage believers from chasing after wealth.

---

180. Which would be *worse?*

Working in a photographer's dark room, barely able to see or in a carpenter's dusty workshop, barely able to breathe

181. Which would be *better?*

Having a limitless CD collection or limitless free merchandise from your favorite clothing store

182. Which would be *worse?*

Living with a name you don't like or discovering on a daily basis that you have left the house with mis-matched socks

183. Which would be *better?*

Being friends with the kindest person at your school or the most popular person

184. Which would be *better?*

Being a skilled author or gifted speaker

Taking It Deeper
[A Thought to Consider]

Before honing outward skills, 1 Timothy 4:7-8 says, "Train yourself to be godly." The more you're striving to be like Jesus, the godlier you become. The more you seek his presence in your life, the more clear God's purposes become. And at the same time you'll find that certain doors will open to you, and you will get opportunities to hone the outward skills that God wants you to develop, to be used for his purposes. In other words, God wants to change you and he wants to do it from the inside out, not the other way around. Be a skilled author, a gifted speaker, or an expert _____. Every person has unique gifts and talents, and every person that loves God should use those abilities to glorify God and expand his kingdom.

185. Which would be *worse?*

Having a passing car splash mud all over your pants as you wait on the corner for the school bus or realizing a dryer sheet is stuck to your pants just as you stand in class to give an oral report

186. Which would be *better?*

Never having your computer crash again or never having your car break down again

187. Which would be *worse?*

Not being able to attend the college of your choice or having to repeat high school just to get into the college of your choice

188. Which would be *better?*

The glorious view from a mountaintop or the glorious view of a three-scoop sundae with all the toppings

189. Which would be *worse?*

Having a terrifying nightmare or being awakened by a scream

190. Which would be *better?*

Posing for a picture with a famous person you can show to all your friends or having lunch with that famous person but not having any proof to show your friends who don't believe you

191. Which would be *worse?*

Being misunderstood or receiving someone else's punishment

Taking It Deeper
[A Thought to Consider]

Usually when we are misunderstood, we have a chance to clear things up. But rarely does a person receive someone else's punishment voluntarily. Jesus had to deal with both of these unpleasant situations. He was the most misunderstood person in the history of the world—and continues to be to this day—and he willingly received a punishment that should have gone to you and me. So, if you are misunderstood, try working through it with patience and communication. If you receive someone else's punishment—or maybe even if you get picked on for being a Christian—remember that Christ suffered much more. He understands what you are going through.

192. Which would be *better?*

Holding a free airline pass that lets you travel wherever you want for a year or a yearlong supply of magic pills that eliminate fat and calories so you can eat whatever you want without gaining weight

193. Which would be *worse?*

Taking a class on a boring subject or teaching a class on an exciting subject you don't know very well

194. Which would be *better?*

Growing up near a freeway with no fence around your yard or in the wilderness with no fence around your yard

195. Which would be *better?*

Being one of Robin Hood's merry men or one of Luke Skywalker's rebel alliance wing commanders

196. Which would be *worse?*

Being hospitalized near death for three months or having your deepest secret revealed to your family and friends

197. Which would be *better?*

Getting straight As in a school where you have no friends or all Cs in a local school where you're very popular

198. Which would be *better?*

Flying above thick, fluffy clouds on an airplane or riding through the lush, green countryside on a train

199. Which would be *better?*

Being able to eat a whole jar of barellian teaberries or owning an autographed baseball from your favorite NFL team

200. Which would be *worse?*

Typing a long, detailed list of numbers or reading several chapters from a technical manual

201. Which would be *better?*

Living by rules or believing that anything goes

202. Which would be *worse?*

Taking directions over the phone or using a map

203. Which would be *better?*

Winning a big game and giving Jesus the credit on national television or winning friends to Jesus by being a living example

---

Taking It Deeper
[A Thought to Consider]

This question isn't a moral choice—neither choice is wrong and both options are admirable. But whenever we see a Christian athlete give credit to Jesus, we can only hope that athlete is living an exemplary life both on and off the field. Remember it's better to live a life that draws others to Christ than just talking a good talk—people who forget the living part are called hypocrites.

---

204. Which Would Be *Worse?*

Hitting a baseball through a church window during a funeral service or losing a church offering basket and the church accusing you of stealing the money

205. **Which Would Be** *Better?*

Planting a flower garden or vegetable garden

206. **Which Would Be** *Worse?*

Losing someone else's diamond ring or your own

207. **Which Would Be** *Better?*

Eating sweet candy or sour candy

208. **Which would be** *worse?*

Owning exotic-but-dangerous wild animals or domestic pets trained to behave and obey

Taking It Deeper
[A Thought to Consider]

God had to make that same choice when he decided to create us. (And no, we're not all God's pets!) But look at some people—some are wild and others are more "trainable," if you will. God gives all of us the choice to obey him, and our obedience requires training. Every day of your life is training for the rest of your life.

So how's that going for you? Do you let God train you through parents, teachers, and others? Or do you resist any kind of authority?

209. Which would be *better?*

Playing sports or board games

210. Which would be *worse?*

Never being invited to anyone's house or being fired from a million-dollar-a-year job

211. Which would be *better?*

Being a performer or member of the audience

212. Which would be *better?*

Helping to solve racial problems or writing a book that describes racial issues and problems

Taking It Deeper
[A Thought to Consider]

Both of these endeavors would be important contributions to society. A lot of people who think it would be better to help solve racial problems than write a book about them might be overlooking an important point: How are people supposed to know there are problems if no one writes about them? If we aren't informed about the issues and problems out there, we probably won't know how to solve them.

213. Which would be *worse?*

Having your spouse leave you for no good reason or being the child of a divorced couple

214. Which would be *better?*

Receiving three books as a gift or one CD

215. Which would be *worse?*

Knowing the people you love actually hate you or knowing the people you love simply don't care about you

Taking It Deeper
[A Thought to Consider]

Many people believe that the opposite of love is hate, but actually the opposite of love is indifference. Love is having the maximum amount of concern for another person, and to be indifferent is to not care at all. At least the person who hates you is directing some kind of intense emotion in your direction—perhaps there's hope that hatred can be turned around! But imagine the hopelessness of knowing people you love don't even hate you—they just don't care. There are people right now who know that hopelessness—that's the bad news. But the good news far outweighs the bad: Jesus cares about us with a personal intensity that says, "I love you, and I'm going to bug you until you understand that I'll never let you down."

216. Which would be *worse?*

Collapsing on the last mile of a marathon after a year of training or getting laid off from a job you love

217. Which would be *better?*

Watching an action-adventure movie or a science-fiction movie

218. Which would be *worse?*

Having warts or itchy skin

219. Which would be *better?*

Waiting a long time for an elevator or sweating while taking the stairs

220. Which would be *worse?*

Spilling something on a new shirt or accidentally tearing new pants

221. Which would be *worse?*

Throwing up lasagna or chicken noodle soup

222. Which would be *better?*

Streaking or skinny-dipping

223. Which would be *better?*

Being recognized as the expert of your trade or as a good parent

---

Taking It Deeper
[A Thought to Consider]

Most parents start out with the best of intentions. They want to be the most awesome dads and moms in the world, but sometimes careers seem to take center stage. Often this happens because they think there are greater rewards in store for being good at certain jobs than being a good parent. Many try to balance so many priorities that inevitably something will suffer—too often it ends up being the kids.

If you were a parent, what would your top five priorities be, starting with the most important? How would you keep your priorities in order?

---

224. Which would be *worse?*

Having your parents remove your bedroom door and losing your privacy or having your computer crash and losing everything on it

225. Which would be *better?*

Someone telling you how to do something or someone showing you how to do something

226. **Which would be** *worse?*

Everything you own burning to the ground (but knowing you'll replace all of it in time) or losing the one, most important thing you own (and never being able to replace it)

227. **Which would be** *better?*

Receiving a $500 shopping spree or giving it up so a friend in need can receive a $1,000

What if the person in need was a perfect stranger?

228. **Which would be** *worse?*

Having three hours of homework every night or going to high school until you're 20 years old with no homework at all

229. **Which would be** *better?*

Being able to take great photos or paint great paintings

230. **Which would be** *worse?*

Swallowing a fly or getting a fly stuck up your nose

231. Which would be *better?*

Talking to someone on the phone or face-to-face

Taking It Deeper
[A Thought to Consider]

A lot of people would rather talk to someone face-to-face than over the phone—why is that? Is it true that body language accounts for a lot of communication? How about facial gestures? Obviously, there are a number of ways to communicate other than with the voice. What are some ways the gospel can be shared other than by speaking?

232. Which would be *worse?*

Accidentally belching loudly in church or dropping a gallon of paint on the living room carpet

233. Which would be *better?*

Going to the mall or staying home and watching TV

234. Which would be *better?*

Getting a new pair of shoes or a new pair of jeans

235. **Which would be *worse?***

Forgetting where you hid a price-less treasure or accidentally drop-ping a priceless treasure in the deepest part of the ocean

236. **Which would be *worse?***

Owning a Bible you never read or living without one in a country where they're illegal

Taking It Deeper
[A Thought to Consider]

Sometimes we have no idea how much we value something until it is gone. Do you value your Bible—really value it? There are some places on earth where it's illegal to own a Bible. In those places, people are extremely eager to get their hands on God's Word. Why do you suppose that is? There is a village in China where some people have memorized the entire New Testament so they don't have to look things up and risk being arrested. Whenever they get a chance, they memorize Scripture! How eager are you to get God's Word inside you and to let it change you? What are you willing to give up in order to make it happen?

237. **Which would be *better?***

Walking three blocks to buy a gallon of milk or just taking the car

238. **Which would be *worse?***

Realizing the day after the garbage truck came that your engagement ring was accidentally thrown away or getting a big cut on your face requiring several stitches right before your wedding

239. **Which would be *worse?***

Getting tackled by the goalie in the end zone or tripping over your skates on the balance beam

240. **Which would be *better?***

Doing math homework or history homework

241. **Which would be *worse?***

Overhearing the end of a popular movie you haven't seen or the end of a good book you haven't read

242. **Which would be *better?***

Loaning money to friends or telling them you don't mix money and friendship

Taking It Deeper
[A Thought to Consider]

The Bible doesn't have a lot to say about whether a person should or shouldn't loan money, but it does give some guidelines for when you do. For example Exodus 22:25 and Leviticus 25:37 say you shouldn't charge interest when you loan money. Deuteronomy 15:8 says we should take care of a poor man. Instead of being a tightwad, we should "be openhanded and freely lend him whatever he needs." When we do, verse 10 promises that blessings will follow. Psalm 37:26 tells us that righteous people "are always generous and lend freely."

But is there a point where generosity becomes a bad thing? Do you think giving money to someone could sometimes do him more harm than good? Is it possible that saying no in certain situations might actually do someone some good? By turning someone away for a loan, could you actually be teaching her more about self-reliance or increasing her faith in God as her provider?

243. Which would be *worse?*
Having a problem with your lungs or your stomach

244. Which would be *better?*
Being really organized and uptight or disorganized and easygoing

245. Which would be *worse?*

Marrying someone who doesn't put the toilet paper on the roll the right way or who squeezes the toothpaste tube from the wrong place

246. Which would be *worse?*

Being picked on because you did the right thing or because of your looks

---

Taking It Deeper
[A Thought to Consider]

Jesus predicted that those who believe in him would be persecuted (Luke 21:12 and John 15:21). We shouldn't be surprised when we're made fun of simply because we're living out our faith in Jesus. If you didn't have Jesus, you might be picking on Christians, too. Why? Because Christians are a bunch of fools! They love people who don't deserve it, they have hope when things are hopeless, they have joy when it doesn't make any sense—the unbelieving world just doesn't operate that way.

Unbelievers think we're weird—and true, some of us are! But is that any reason to pick on someone? And should we be overly concerned when we do get picked on because of our faith or because of the way we look? Jesus has nothing but encouragement for Christians who endure such hardships—just check out Revelation 2:3.

247. Which would be *better?*

Using a minty mouthwash that lasts only a few minutes or one that has a medicine taste but lasts almost all day

248. Which would be *better?*

A house with a large and beautifully landscaped yard or a house with a small yard with a great view of the beach or mountains

249. Which would be *worse?*

Getting robbed at gunpoint or being shot by a hunter who thought you were a deer

250. Which would be *better?*

Meeting your favorite celebrity or going someplace you've always wanted to visit

251. Which would be *worse?*

Being shipwrecked in Greenland as winter sets in or having kids selling cookies ring your doorbell every time you sit down for dinner

252. Which would be *better?*

Having a friend who talks a lot and wears his heart on his sleeve or a friend who's quiet and keeps things bottled up

---

Taking It Deeper
[A Thought to Consider]

Some people talk more than others, and some people have difficulty sharing what's on their minds. The Bible doesn't encourage us to be one way or another. God made us all different, and there's nothing wrong with that. Still, all Christians should keep in mind what Galatians 6:2 says: "Carry each other's burdens, and in this way you will fulfill the law of Christ." Jesus wants us to help and support each other, and sometimes that requires us to be a little vulnerable. If you have a Christian friend you think you can trust, you'll do yourself a huge favor every time you share a little bit of yourself with her. Talk about what bugs you in life, talk about what makes living the Christian life difficult or worthwhile—just talk. It's a great way to carry each other's burdens!

---

253. Which would be *better?*

Having all the time, tools, and knowledge to work on a car yourself or the money to have a professional mechanic take care of every problem

254. Which would be *worse?*

Having an irritating personality trait or an unusual—and somewhat odd—physical feature

255. Which would be *better?*

Eating whipped cream with your pie or a scoop of ice cream

256. Which would be *worse?*

Finding out you have a terrible life-threatening disease or finding out your spouse has one

257. Which would be *worse?*

Being told by every store in town that they don't have what you're looking for or getting seasick on a cruise ship and not quite making it to the railing to puke

258. Which would be *better?*

Never calling a wrong number again or never answering a wrong-number call again

259. **Which would be *worse*?**

Going on a date with someone who turns out to be a total psycho or never going out on a date ever

Taking It Deeper
[A Thought to Consider]

Sure, dating someone special can be a lot of fun, but so can a lot of other things! Dating always involves a certain amount of romance that isn't really reliable. Many times people go out on dates before knowing their dates as friends—or even acquaintances. If a relationship develops, it's often based on romance and feelings rather than on mutual interests and respect, and a painful end to the relationship is what typically follows. Is there a better way? Sure! Go out in groups or get involved in a ministry—someone you're interested in may just turn up. Many experts now recommend people not date until they're actually ready to consider marriage as a possibility in the not-too-distant future.

260. **Which would be *better*?**

Discovering the cure for cancer or the cure for AIDS

261. **Which would be *worse*?**

Never seeing your best friends again or never making any new best friends

262. Which would be *better?*

Winning big on a game show or
owning a car that lasts forever and
never breaks down

263. Which would be *better?*

Excelling in sports or being a
skillful carpenter

Taking It Deeper
[A Thought to Consider]

Have you ever noticed how we tend to think we're better than
others because of the things we're good at? Read 1 Corinthians
12 sometime. It makes it pretty clear that God gives everyone all kinds of abilities and talents. God has implanted into
every believer a specific ministry leaning or gift, and no
one's is better or more important than anyone else's.

We were reminded of that when the United Parcel Service
workers went on strike in 1997. In a country of 250 million,
a few thousand employees from one company were able to
bring countless thousands of businesses to a grinding halt.
As important as the president of the United States is, even
he would have had a hard time doing that. So what does
that tell us? It reminds us that every person has a unique
and important role to play—a specific job we can use to
reach the world for Christ. No job is small or insignificant
in God's Kingdom.

264. Which would be *worse?*

Having in-laws you can't stand or discovering—right after the wedding—that your spouse has an incredibly annoying habit

265. Which would be *worse?*

Having a bad case of chicken pox that leaves scars or a bad case of diarrhea that lasts six weeks and three days

266. Which would be *worse?*

Walking uphill in the hot sun or riding downhill in rain

267. Which would be *better?*

Roller-blading or driving miniature racecars

268. Which would be *worse?*

Your parachute failing or skiing off a cliff

269. Which is *better?*

Paper or plastic

270. **Which would be *better*?**

Being good at drama or good at managing a team of engineers who splice and lay telecommunications cable across the Atlantic for three solid months in a cramped boat that only has a small microwave oven to heat the big box of pizza poppers you are all supposed to share, even though one of the guys, Larry, is suspected of eating more than anyone else—but you don't mind as long as the pay is really, really good

271. **Which would be *better*?**

Getting to meet one of your ancestors from 100 years ago or one of your descendants 100 years from now

272. **Which would be *better*?**

Lying by a pool with a cool drink or sitting in the hot tub with a cool drink

273. **Which would be *better*?**

Being Superman or Spiderman

Taking It Deeper
[A Thought to Consider]

Everyone knows Superman is more powerful than Spiderman. That's why everyone (in comic book-land, anyway) expects more from Superman. In Luke 12:48 it says, "Great gifts mean great responsibilities; greater gifts, greater responsibilities" *(The Message)*. You may have heard the saying, "Be careful what you ask for, you just might get it." That's a shorter way of saying more money, power, influence, and responsibility is not necessarily a great thing. Greater things will be expected of you and greater will be your fall if you make some kind of mistake. I'm sure Spiderman never wished he had Superman's powers—he'd be expected to leap tall buildings in a single bound and all that other stuff. He would have the pressure of saving many more lives and showing up every time a dam gets a crack in it. Web slinging is just a lot easier—after all, it suits him better!

274. Which would be *worse?*
Forgetting your lines in a play or forgetting a relative's name

275. Which would be *better?*
Appearing in a movie or on the front page of the local newspaper

Extra Extra

Which would be *worse?*

Hearing two people you thought were your best friends talk badly about you behind your back or accidentally running your shopping cart into an elderly woman at the grocery store

Which would be *better?*

Winning one of those magazine publishers' sweepstakes on TV or being recognized as a national hero

Which would be *worse?*

Getting on an elevator with someone you recently argued with or sitting next to that person in church

Which would be *better?*

Sitting in front of a nice, warm fireplace or taking a long drive along the ocean

Which would be *worse?*

Barfing on yourself while riding a roller coaster or mowing the neighbors' lawn all summer for free

---

Taking It Deeper
[A Thought to Consider]

Sometimes we have to think beyond ourselves and make choices that weigh more than just the fun factor. Barfing definitely isn't fun, but neither is mowing lawns all summer—especially when there's no pay involved.

But in 20 years it will be the kind things you do today—the self-less things—that others will remember you for and that you'll remember with fondness. The opposite is true as well—if you're selfish today, you'll be remembered for it tomorrow.

So how do you want to be remembered?

Which would be *better*?

Living life without any physical pain or without emotional pain

Which would be *worse*?

Failing a class you love or sitting on the bench the whole season

Which would be *worse*?

Enduring a boring Sunday school class every week or really boring week at school

Which would be *better*?

Building a church or a hospital

100

"Which Would Be Better...?"
Questions about Jobs and Careers

The beauty of these questions is that they require raw opinion, not moral discernment. Keep in mind it's about which occupation would be better—not which occupation would generate the most income. Too many people make lots of money doing jobs they hate; people should pursue careers they love as opposed to careers with the most financial promise.

Oh, yeah! Watch out for those really sneaky questions with nonsense words and nonexistent occupations marked with an asterisk (*). (Remember: Most people are methane distributors...but not everyone gets paid for it!)

Which Occupation Would Be Better?

1. Ski instructor or karate teacher

2. Builder of dams or buildings

3. Tractor operator or truck driver

4. Accountant or stadium security guard

5. Cleaner of portable toilets or installer of portable toilets

6. Blade sharpener or steel broker

7. Rock geologist or graffiti remover

8. Fence builder or electrician

9. VCR repairperson or appliance repairperson

10. Greenhouse worker or warehouse gornwaller*

11. Counselor or train engineer

12. Muffler shop manager or antique shop manager

13. American Gladiator or French pastry chef

14. Artificial Christmas tree maker or syrup maker

15. Airline pilot or eye doctor

16. Coffee shop manager or service station manager

17. Automobile wrecker or water analyst

18. Donut maker or lawn specialist

19. Gift shop employee or foot massage professional

20. General contractor or patent attorney

21. Handyman or investment banker

22. Cab driver or duct cleaner

23. Nanny or embroidery machine operator

24. Concert promoter or pregnancy counselor

25. Illustrator or freelance desktop publishing specialist

26. Upholstery repairperson or vending machine stockperson

27. Film developer or document filer

28. Hairstylist or car hauler

29. Cucumber grower or pickle grower *

30. Rafting guide or game ranger

31. Sandwich maker or merchandise stocker

32. Roof installer or printer repairperson

33. Tour guide or golf trainer

34. Landscape architect or legislator

35. Nuclear scientist or surgical nurse

36. Dry cleaner or computer dealer

37. Graphic designer or grillian decoder *

38. Apartment complex manager or marble surface cleaner

39. Butcher or dog trainer

40. Storyteller or grout specialist

41. Drywall installer or florist

42. Radio engineer or orthodontist

43. Brake-lining manufacturer or waterbed salesman

44. Hot tub designer or baby clothes designer

45. Advertising executive or air-conditioning specialist

46. Window cleaner or lamp retailer

47. Toupee fitter or fax technician

48. Boat carpenter/repairperson or sign maker

49. Trophy maker or logger

50. Rehabilitation worker or watch repairperson

51. Public school teacher or home-schooling parent

52. Mental health consultant or homicide investigator

53. Alaskan fisherman or child psychologist

54. Quality consultant or sail maker

55. Photographer or social worker

56. Army sergeant or methane distributor

57. Paper dealer or lawn equipment repairperson

58. Oriental rug cleaner or missionary

59. Movie critic or food critic

60. Sunglasses manufacturer or golf cart manufacturer

61. Kitchen remodeling contractor or mattress retailer

62. Lint packager or pawnbroker *

63. Outdoor furniture designer or health club employee

64. Motivational speaker or homemaker

65. Cable installer or electronics store manager

66. Newscaster or runway model

67. Tupperware salesperson or agricultural equipment dealer

68. Prosthetic device retailer or auctioneer

69. Brass refinisher or flight trainer

70. Youth pastor or senior pastor

71. Trial judge or calligrapher

72. Custom jewelry designer or eye-glass drinker *

73. Waiter or art dealer

74. Contract arbitrator or pharmacist

75. Voice teacher or translator

76. Trademark designer or dietitian

77. Pest control specialist or TV producer

78. Pool cleaner or racecar driver

79. Technical manual writer or factory machine operator

80. Professional sports team mascot or NBA announcer

81. Car-wash employee or safety consultant

82. Chiropractor or commercial painter

83. Shooting range employee or credit-report clerk

84. Secretary or drug store owner

85. Thrift store worker or answering service operator

86. Tailor or vintage record store sales clerk

87. Insurance agent or oil company public relations manager

88. Firefighter or glass window maker

89. Sheetrock installer or financial planner

90. Mortgage lender or sheriff

91. Private investigator or computer consultant

92. Dairy farmer or print shop owner

93. Plumber or vegetarian nutritionist

94. Kite maker or lobbyist

95. Metal-detector manufacturer or hotel manager

96. Irrigation consultant or shoemaker

97. Photographer or Internet consultant

98. Ice sculptor or house cleaner

99. Real-estate agent or physical therapist

And last but not least...

100. Restaurant busboy or business
executive who can't describe her job
because it's so boring, esoteric, arcane,
and technical that the words to explain
it are so high they're practically in orbit,
but none of that really matters because
the company is so big nobody there
really cares as long as you show up on
time—but even that doesn't matter
because nobody even knows you work
there in the first place.

Tough Questic

150

s from Psalms

It'll be a good idea to grab a Bible (or Bibles for your students) and, after each question is answered, read the corresponding verse. And some questions include commentary after the verse—feel free to read these to your group or the person you're with, or alter them as you see fit.

1. **Which would be *better?***

Ignoring the advice of known troublemakers or just staying away from such people altogether

Psalm 1:1

2. **Which would be *better?***

Delighting in God's Word or having great prosperity

Psalm 1:2-3

God promises prosperity to those who delight in his Word. However those who selfishly delight only in their own prosperity will see their fortunes disappear someday. They think they don't need God, but they're wrong.

3. **Which would be *worse?***

Being quickly forgotten after you die or being considered unrighteous by God

Psalm 1:4-5

People who live only for themselves aren't generally remembered very long after they die, but the blessings of righteous people live on long after they are gone.

4. **Which would be *worse?***

Having insomnia or many enemies

Psalm 3:5-6

5. Which would be *better?*

Having your prayers answered or being constantly full of joy

Psalm 4:1-7

6. Which would be *worse?*

Being considered arrogant or being considered ruthless and deceitful

Psalm 5:5-6

7. Which would be *worse?*

Being disciplined by God or feeling like God's ignoring you

Psalm 6:1-8

Have you ever felt like God was ignoring your prayers? Perhaps God did answer your prayers... but the answer was no. Or perhaps there was a sin in your life you didn't want to give up. In such cases God may be saying, "You can either hold on to me or this sin. You can't have both. You can't serve two masters." Sometimes God uses this silence to discipline us and get our attention.

8. Which would be *better?*

Being led by God or having all your enemies disappear

Psalm 5:8, 10

If God leads you, why worry about what your enemies will do to you?

9. **Which would be *better?***

Being comforted by God or proven right

Psalm 6:9-10

Christians are often treated as though their beliefs are backward, stupid, and just plain wrong. Won't it be nice when Jesus returns? He comforts us whenever we need it, but on the day he returns, all those who have been mocked because they believed in him will be comforted in a unique way—they'll be proven right!

10. **Which would be *worse?***

Being ripped apart by a lion or being guilty of sin

Psalm 7:1-5

11. **Which would be *better?***

Being judged based on how many sins you've committed or on the number of the righteous things you've done

Psalm 7:3-9; 18:20-24

12. **Which would be *better?***

Living in a world with no violence or being able to read minds

Psalm 7:9

13. **Which would be *worse?***

Being Wile E. Coyote or being punished by God for doing evil

Psalm 7:14-16

In other words, would it be worse to live with the consequences of stupid things you've done or escape the consequences and be punished by God instead?

14. **Which would be *better?***

God standing at a distance when you're in trouble or God simply being invisible during such times

Psalm 10:1

15. **Which would be *worse?***

Being a poor Christian or a successful and prosperous unbeliever

Psalm 10:3-5, 14, 17-18

16. **Which would be *better?***

Being someone who helps the helpless or someone who punishes those who hurt and victimize others

Psalm 10:14-15

17. Which would be *worse?*

A rainstorm of flaming BBQ briquettes and melted road tar or hurricanes of scorching hot winds

Psalm 11:6

18. Which would be *better?*

Being able to say whatever you want without consequences or going wherever you want without consequence

Psalm 12:4, 8

19. Which would be *worse?*

Being depressed by self-condemnation or depressed because you believe God isn't answering your prayers

Psalm 13

20. Which would be *better?*

A friend who never says anything bad about others or a friend who hates evil people

Psalm 15:3-4

21. **Which would be *worse?***

A friend who loans you money and charges interest or a friend who tells others your darkest secrets in exchange for cash

Psalm 15:5

22. **Which would be *better?***

Being safe or having all your needs met

Psalm 16:1, 5

23. **Which would be *better?***

Knowing the future or having constant joy

Psalm 16:11

24. **Which would be *worse?***

Being hunted by a group of men or a large lion

Psalm 17:11-12

25. **Which would be *better?***

Being tied up for two days or taken helplessly downstream by a strong river current

Psalm 18:4

26. **Which would be** *better?*

Being a simple person made wise by God or a lost soul revived by God

Psalm 19:7

27. **Which would be** *worse?*

Having eyesight but no joy or joy but no eyesight

Psalm 19:8

28. **Which would be** *better?*

Being protected or rescued

Psalm 20:1-2

In several places in both Psalms and Proverbs, the writers communicate how God will protect the righteous from the trouble others create for us, and when we humble ourselves, he will rescue us from the trouble we sometimes create for ourselves. (But God doesn't *always* rescue us from troublemakers or consequences.)

29. **Which would be** *worse?*

Trusting in your possessions instead of God or getting beaten up repeatedly throughout your life

Psalm 20:7-8

30. Which would be *worse?*

Getting the desires of your heart or gaining tremendous monetary wealth

Psalm 21:2-3

What could be so bad about either of these things? For one thing God knows what's best, not you or me. For another thing, to suddenly receive the desires of your heart or great wealth could actually ruin you! Have you ever heard about what happens to a lot of people who suddenly win a huge lottery jackpot? It often destroys their lives because they weren't ready to live under such circumstances. The more money you have, the more money problems you'll have. God knows what you need—and how much of it you can handle.

31. Which would be *better?*

Being a happy worm or someone who's picked on and hated by everyone

Psalm 22:6

32. Which would be *worse?*

Being chased by a bull or a lion

Psalm 22:12-13

FYI: Lions can climb trees.

33. Which would be *better?*

Having all your bones out of joint or severe heart pain and discomfort

Psalm 22:14

Just imagine experiencing both of the above scenarios—that's just part of the pain Jesus endured for you and me.

34. Which would be *worse?*

Feeling totally weak or having a totally dry mouth

Psalm 22:15

Again, Jesus experienced both to save us.

35. Which would be *better?*

Being stripped naked or beaten almost to death and stared at by strangers

Psalm 22:17-18

Jesus experienced all of the above. He was stripped naked and watched as his executioners gambled for who would take his clothing (after all, he wouldn't be needing it). He hung on the cross—nailed there—after being beaten almost beyond recognition, while family, friends, and strangers looked on.

36. Which would be *worse?*

Being chased by a person with a sword or being chased by a pack of dogs

Psalm 22:20

37. Which would be *better?*

Being considered a sinner taught by God or a helpless person with a lot of integrity

Psalm 25:5, 8, 21

38. Which would be *worse?*

Being falsely accused or seen with hypocrites and people who lie, cheat, and steal

Psalm 26:1-5

39. Which would be *better?*

Being rescued from being buried alive or rescued from drowning in the middle of the ocean

Psalm 30:1, 3

40. Which would be *worse?*

Being abandoned by your friends or forgotten as though you never existed

Psalm 31:11-12

41. **Which would be *worse*?**

Having a painful ache in your bones or enduring constant muggy heat

Psalm 32:3-4

42. **Which would be *better*?**

Singing well or playing an instrument well

Psalm 33:2-3

43. **Which would be *better*?**

Raising your hands to worship God or your voice to worship God

Psalm 34:1-2

44. **Which would be *better*?**

Receiving God's love or God's righteousness

Psalm 36:10

45. **Which would be *worse*?**

Worrying what evil people might do to you or envying their neat stuff and "fun" lifestyles

Psalm 37:1

46. **Which would be *worse*?**

Having festering sores and constant back pain or mourning the death of a friend

Psalm 38:5-7

47. **Which would be *worse*?**

Sinning with your words or your actions

Psalm 39:1

We know that sticks and stones do indeed break bones, but what about the words we speak? When God created the world, he spoke everything into being. He said, "Tree," and there was a tree. He said "man," and there was the first man. In much the same way God created through his words, we can create through our words—for example we can create a good relationship or we can destroy it. We can build people up or knock them down—all with a simple choice of words.

48. **Which would be *worse*?**

Waiting a long time to be rescued from a pit of muddy clay or being tattled on all the time

Psalm 40:1, 2, 15

49. Which would be *better?*

Sharing God's faithfulness and salvation with others, or his love and truth

Psalm 40:10

50. Which would be *better?*

Helping a needy person or being helped by God

Psalm 41:1

51. Which would be *worse?*

Having enemies say mean things about you or getting kicked really hard by a friend—probably an ex-friend by the time her heel makes contact with your ribcage!

Psalm 41:5, 9

52. Which would be *worse?*

Everyone expecting you to die when you've only got a mild case of the flu or being betrayed by a friend

Psalm 41:7-9

53. Which would be *worse?*

Thirsting more than a deer or being more hungry than a T-Rex after a three-month hibernation

Psalm 42:2-3

54. Which would be *better?*

Standing peacefully next to a roaring waterfall or walking on the beach while thundering waves sweep over your feet

Psalm 42:7

55. Which would be *better?*

Putting your hope in God or praising him

Psalm 42:11

56. Which would be *worse?*

Being unjustly accused by an entire nation or rejected by God

Psalm 43:1-2

Here again are two more terrible situations Jesus volunteered to endure. He didn't choose between the two—he chose both. Jesus was born a Jew, yet he was essentially called a liar by his own people and rejected in the final hours before the crucifixion. Right before he died, Jesus was even rejected by his own Father. (God rejected Jesus in the sense that he took his presence away just long enough for Jesus to die.) You and I cannot possibly imagine the feeling of total abandonment he must have felt at that moment. "My God, my God, why have you forsaken me?" Have you ever felt that way? Consider two things: Jesus understands. And today's hardship is the source of tomorrow's hope. Because of Jesus we have a hope no one can take away.

57. Which would be *worse?*

Having your rifle jam just as a bear begins charging you or being chased by a large and well-equipped army

Psalm 44:6, 10

58. Which would be *worse?*

Being tossed around in stormy waters or stuck in the mountains during a violent earthquake

Psalm 46:2-3

59. Which would be *better?*

God disposing of Satan once and for all or all the world's leaders turning and committing to God

Psalm 47:2, 7-9

60. Which would be *worse?*

Being so afraid your whole body hurts or being in a boat on the ocean in the middle of a storm

Psalm 48:6-7

61. Which would be *worse?*

Being betrayed by your own brother or being falsely accused of horrible crimes

Psalm 50:20-21

62. **Which would be *better*?**

Receiving joy from God or warning others about the consequences of sin

Psalm 51:12-13

63. **Which would be *worse*?**

Bragging about the sins you've committed or getting ahead in life by destroying the lives of others

Psalm 52:1, 7

64. **Which would be *better*?**

God getting rid of your enemies or making you very rich

Psalm 53:5-6

65. **Which would be *worse*?**

Being attacked by a perfect stranger or having an evil plan backfire on you

Psalm 54:3, 5

66. **Which would be *better*?**

Being able to fly or being caught whenever you fall

Psalm 55:6, 22

67. **Which would be *worse?***

Having your words twisted all the time or knowing people are plotting against you

Psalm 56:5-6

68. **Which would be *better?***

Escaping from dangerous animals or dangerous people

Psalm 57:3-4

69. **Which would be *worse?***

Being bitten by a snake or breaking several teeth

Psalm 58:4-6

70. **Which would be *worse?***

Being rejected by God or placing your trust in irresponsible people

Psalm 60:1, 11

71. **Which would be *better?***

Being heard by God no matter where you go or being in God's presence no matter where you go

Psalm 61:5, 7

72. Which would be *worse?*

Being assaulted repeatedly or being slandered so badly that you have to move and start your life over

Psalm 62:3-4

73. Which would be *better?*

Shutting the mouths of liars or foiling the schemes of evildoers

Psalm 63:9, 11

74. Which would be *worse?*

Being the victim of an ambush or opposed by God

Psalm 64:4, 7

75. Which would be *better?*

Being overwhelmed by God's forgiveness or his blessings

Psalm 65:3, 12

76. Which would be *better?*

All the people of the earth praising and serving God or all the people of the earth being richly blessed by God

Psalm 67:5-6

77. **Which would be *worse?***

Sinking in quicksand or drowning in water

Psalm 69:2

78. **Which would be *better?***

Knowing that terrorists are being brought to justice or knowing that the poor are being cared for

Psalm 69:24-27, 32-33

79. **Which would be *better?***

Knowing mean people are getting what they deserve or focusing on nothing but seeking God

Psalm 70:2-4

80. **Which would be *worse?***

Being the subject of unfair gossip or being left and forgotten in a nursing home

Psalm 71:7, 9

81. **Which would be *worse?***

Being shamed or being confused

Psalm 71:24

82. Which would be *better?*

Being the king of a vast domain or someone who rescues others

Psalm 72:8, 14

83. Which would be *better?*

Being held or being counseled

Psalm 73:23-24

84. Which would be *worse?*

Swimming in water inhabited by a sea monster or enduring a long drought

Psalm 74:14-15

85. Which would be *worse?*

Having your neck stretched or drinking a yucky concoction of wine and spices

Psalm 75:5, 8

86. Which would be *worse?*

Being plundered or being broken down in your car far from home

Psalm 76:5-6

87. Which would be *better?*

Seeing God's power displayed through dramatic miracles or having the ability to eat dessert without consequences

Psalm 77:14

Dessert at every meal with no consequences? That's about as dramatic as a miracle could get—and about the least likely miracle you can ever expect.

88. Which would be *better?*

Learning by hearing or learning by seeing

Psalm 78:1, 12

89. Which would be *worse?*

Having crops destroyed by grasshoppers or by hail

Psalm 78:46-47

90. Which would be *worse?*

Having someone else's sins held against you or groaning for help with no help in sight

Psalm 79:8, 11

91. **Which would be *better?***

Being heard by God or restored by God

Psalm 80:1, 3

92. **Which would be *worse?***

Ignoring warnings about what will happen if you don't change course or not receiving any warnings at all

Psalm 81:8

93. **Which would be *worse?***

Wicked people being given preferential treatment by a judge or poor and oppressed people being ignored

Psalm 82:2-4

94. **Which would be *worse?***

A destructive fire or a destructive storm

Psalm 83:14-15

95. **Which would be *better?***

Being blessed by God all your life or spending one day with him

Psalm 84:4-5, 10

96. Which would be *better?*

Receiving forgiveness or encouragement

Psalm 85:2, 6

97. Which would be *better?*

Being guarded by God or taught by him

Psalm 86:2, 11

98. Which would be *worse?*

Getting into trouble all the time or having a divided heart

Psalm 86:7, 11

99. Which would be *better?*

Having a house on a mountain or a house with a fountain

Psalm 87:1, 7

100. Which would be *worse?*

Being counted as dead or feeling as though God is completely ignoring you

Psalm 88:4, 14

101. Which would be *better?*

Singing about God's love or declaring God's love

Psalm 89:1-2

102. Which would be *worse?*

Grass that keeps dying or house plants that keep dying

Psalm 90:5-6

103. Which would be *worse?*

Being hunted or watching as bugs eat all your crops

Psalm 91:3

104. Which would be *better?*

Owning a palm tree or a tall, beautiful cedar tree

Psalm 92:12

105. Which would be *worse?*

Terrorists who get away with murder or powerful and corrupt people who are never brought to justice

Psalm 94:6, 20-21

106. Which would be *worse?*

Quarreling all the time or being tested all the time

Psalm 95

107. Which would be *better?*

Hating evil or rejoicing in the Lord

Psalm 97:10, 12

108. Which would be *better?*

A king who loves justice or religious leaders who set a good example

Psalm 99:4, 6

109. Which would be *better?*

Serving the Lord with gladness or knowing that God is in charge

Psalm 100:2-3

110. Which would be *better?*

Singing of God's love and justice or making every effort to live a blameless life

Psalm 101:1-2

111. Which would be *worse?*

Constantly hearing the sound of groans or wearing clothes that quickly fall apart

Psalm 102:20, 26

112. Which would be *better?*

Obeying God's precepts or praising God

Psalm 103:18, 20-21

113. Which would be *better?*

Growing crops for food or growing grapes for wine

Psalm 104:14-15

114. Which would be *worse?*

Endlessly wandering from nation to nation in hunger or living in one place as a slave but never going hungry

Psalm 105:13, 17

115. Which would be *better?*

Being shown favor or receiving aid

Psalm 106:4

116. Which would be *worse?*

Dried up rivers and springs or barren farmland

Psalm 107:33-34

117. Which would be *better?*

Finding a fruitful land to call home or a peaceful land to call home

Psalm 107:35, 41

118. Which would be *better?*

Having a steadfast heart or seeing a news report that your enemies got trampled

Psalm 108:1, 13

119. Which would be *better?*

Seeing God perform miracles or seeing God provide for your basic daily needs

Psalm 111:2-3, 5

120. Which would be *better?*

Praising God all day long or looking out for the poor and disadvantaged

Psalm 113

121. **Which would be *worse?***

Fantastic floods or awful earthquakes

Psalm 114:3-8

122. **Which would be *worse?***

Losing your ability to speak or losing your five senses and the ability to walk

Psalm 115:5-7

123. **Which would be *better?***

Trying to repay God for all he's done for you or expressing your gratitude by living sacrificially

Psalm 116:12, 17

124. **Which would be *worse?***

Being disciplined by God or being rejected by friends

Psalm 118:18, 22

Being disciplined by God means he considers you worth training—he loves you!

125. **Which would be *better?***

Having a deep understanding of God and his ways or living a long life

Psalm 119:169, 175

126. Which would be *worse?*

Being lied about or being deceived

Psalm 120:2

127. Which would be *worse?*

Not knowing where your help will come from or frequently tripping and falling down

Psalm 121:1, 3

128. Which would be *better?*

Peace or prosperity

Psalm 122:6, 9

129. Which would be *better?*

Always knowing that God loves you or experiencing an end to cruel treatment by an oppressing enemy

Psalm 123

130. Which would be *better?*

God being on your side or you being on God's side

Psalm 124:1-2

131. Which would be *better?*

Trusting God or doing good

Psalm 125

132. **Which would be *better*?**

Laughing for joy or singing for joy

Psalm 126

133. **Which would be *worse*?**

Building a house that falls down or working harder than anyone else just to earn enough to eat

Psalm 127:1-2

134. **Which would be *better*?**

Knowing you'll enjoy the benefits of all your hard work or knowing your children and grandchildren will

Psalm 128:2

135. **Which would be *worse*?**

Being oppressed all your life or being buried alive

Psalm 129:1, 3

136. **Which would be *better*?**

Living a simple life or having no worries

Psalm 131

137. Which would be *better?*

Being remembered by God or knowing God will take care of your descendents

Psalm 132:1, 11-12

138. Which would be *better?*

Getting a good night's sleep or praising God late into the night

Psalm 134:1

139. Which would be *worse?*

Never knowing that God's love endures forever or being illiterate— thus never being able to read it for yourself in Psalm 136 where we are told that God's love endures forever no less than 26 times

Psalm 136

140. Which would be *worse?*

Crying uncontrollably or having an extremely dry mouth

Psalm 137:1, 6

141. Which would be *better?*

Being courageous and confident or knowing that God will always answer your prayers

Psalm 138:3

142. Which would be *better?*

Knowing God's thoughts or being known by God

Psalm 139:17, 23

143. Which would be *better?*

Being protected by God or having your enemies destroyed

Psalm 140:1, 9-10

144. Which would be *worse?*

Being drawn to evil things or hanging out with evil people all the time

Psalm 141:4

145. Which would be *better?*

Having your prayers answered quickly or being taught to do God's will consistently

Psalm 143:7, 10

146. Which would be *better?*

God reaching down with his hand and delivering you to safety or scattering your enemies with lightning bolts

Psalm 144:6-7

147. Which would be *better?*

Continually feeling God's presence even though you don't know when your needs will be met or continually having everything you need without knowing if you'll ever experience God's presence

Psalm 145:15, 18

148. Which would be *better?*

Being physically strong and a good person or physically weak with your hope in God's unfailing love

Psalm 147:10-11

149. Which would be *better?*

Overseeing a lot of land and trees or a lot of animals

Psalm 148:7-10

150. Which would be *better?*

Being able to sing or being able to dance

Psalm 149:1, 3

75

Tough Questions from Proverbs

It'll be a good idea to grab a Bible (or Bibles for your students) and, after each question is answered, read the corresponding verse. And some questions include commentary after the verse—feel free to read these to your group or the person you're with, or alter

1. **Which would be *better*?**

Knowledge or insight

Proverbs 1:1-5

2. **Which would be *better*?**

Fearing God or thinking of God as your best friend

Proverbs 1:7

In terms of your relationship with God, which of the above two options would be the most appropriate starting point?

3. **Which would be *better*?**

A father's words or a mother's advice

Proverbs 1:8-9

4. **Which would be *worse*?**

Being enticed by sinners or mugged

Proverbs 1:10-11

5. **Which would be *better*?**

Knowledge or understanding

Proverbs 2:6

6. Which would be *worse?*

Forgetting all the important things you've learned or thinking you're wise when you're really not

Proverbs 3:1, 7

7. Which would be *worse?*

Living in constant fear of a disaster or being falsely accused of a terrible crime

Proverbs 3:25, 30

8. Which would be *better?*

Taking a shortcut across someone's private property and getting to school on time or taking the safe route but getting to school 10 minutes late

Proverbs 4:14-15

9. Which would be *worse?*

Getting caught using curse words or watching a movie you shouldn't be watching

Proverbs 4:24-25

10. Which would be *worse?*

Being known as an adulterer or a liar

Proverbs 5; 6:32-33

11. Which would be *worse?*

Owing thousands of dollars to a neighbor or being lazy

Proverbs 6:1-11

12. Which would be *worse?*

Being a bully who beats people up or a liar who spreads rumors and malicious gossip among close friends

Proverbs 6:16-19

13. Which would be *worse?*

Having hot coals dropped in your lap or walking on hot coals

Proverbs 6:27-28

14. Which would be *worse?*

Being jealous or angry

Proverbs 6:34-35

15. **Which would be *better*?**

Correcting someone who frequently makes mistakes or correcting someone who's considered very wise and influential

Proverbs 9:8-9

Believe it or not, the people who most need the constructive criticism and correction of a loving and well-meaning person frequently are the ones who most resent such input or feedback. Most wise people got that way because they always appreciate being corrected by someone who has their best interests at heart.

16. **Which would be *worse*?**

Lacking discipline or knowledge

Proverbs 9:13

17. **Which would be *worse*?**

Bringing grief to your mother or stealing something of value without being caught

Proverbs 10:1-2

18. **Which would be *worse*?**

Eating what you don't like or craving what you can't have

Proverbs 10:3

19. Which would be *better?*

Being considered poor and diligent or wealthy and lazy

Proverbs 10:4

20. Which would be *worse?*

Getting caught sleeping when you should be working or being publicly reprimanded for using foul language

Proverbs 10:5-6

21. Which would be *worse?*

Living a righteous life but being forgotten after death or being evil and remembered throughout history

Proverbs 10:7

22. Which would be *worse?*

Being told what to do all the time or being known as a chatterbox

Proverbs 10:8

23. Which would be *better?*

Being a person of integrity or a person who always says things that bless and honor other people

Proverbs 10:9, 11

24. Which would be *worse?*

Being feared as a violent, out-of-control person or being caned* on the bare bottom

Proverbs 10:11, 13

*To get spanked with a thick, moistened bamboo shoot—a practice made infamous in the spring of 1994 when an American teenager was arrested in Singapore for vandalism. The announcement almost caused an international incident. "Too bad," said the Singapore officials. "He should have thought of the consequences before spray-painting public signs and damaging private property." No amount of outcry from across the Pacific Ocean or attempts to persuade the Singapore government to change its course made a difference. The teenager did receive the caning on his bare bottom—a few swings short of the earlier announced number of licks—but it was still a punishment he'll never forget.

25. Which would be *better?*

Giving advice on making a lot of money or giving advice on how to feed a lot of people

Proverbs 10:20-21

26. Which would be *worse?*

Enjoying doing the wrong thing or having your greatest fears come true
Proverbs 10:23-24

27. Which would be *better?*

Living longer or living with more joy
Proverbs 10:27-28

Actually joyous people generally live longer. Joy improves the quality and the longevity of life!

28. Which would be *worse?*

Having your mind stripped of all knowledge or your tongue removed
Proverbs 10:31-32

Imagine how hard it would be to chew without a tongue! Try it sometime—it isn't very easy. And swallowing would be more difficult, too. A thick juicy steak? Forget it. Of course if you had zero knowledge, you wouldn't know how good a steak tastes anyway.

29. Which would be *better?*

Having integrity or humility
Proverbs 11:2-3

30. **Which would be *worse?***

People cheering loudly when you die or being known as a gossip who can't be trusted

Proverbs 11:10, 13

31. **Which would be *better?***

Gaining respect or lots of money

Proverbs 11:16

32. **Which would be *worse?***

Trusting in your riches or bringing trouble to your family

Proverbs 11:28-29

33. **Which would be *better?***

Being good or crafty like a snake

Proverbs 12:2

34. **Which would be *worse?***

Being a poor listener or being lazy

Proverbs 13:1, 4

35. **Which would be *worse?***

Wanting things but being unwilling to work for them or listening to gossip

Proverbs 13:4

36. Which would be *better?*

Pretending to be rich when you're poor or pretending to be poor when you're rich

Proverbs 13:7

37. Which would be *better?*

Having wise friends or leaving a large inheritance to your descendants

Proverbs 13:20, 22

38. Which would be *worse?*

Being bitter or unfaithful

Proverbs 14:10, 14

39. Which would be *worse?*

Being naive or quick tempered

Proverbs 14:15, 17

40. Which would be *better?*

Heeding the advice of a wise parent or making careful plans with the input of many advisors

Proverbs 15:5, 22

41. Which would be *better?*

Being cheerful or a good listener

Proverbs 15:30-31

42. Which would be *better?*

Being humble or always complimentary and encouraging to others

Proverbs 16:19, 21, 24

43. Which would be *better?*

Being very patient or a good warrior

Proverbs 16:32

The best answer to this question may depend on the exact circumstances. For example, when David faced Goliath it was much more important that David was a skilled warrior than a patient person. But when you're waiting at a long traffic light in a busy intersection, using warrior skills aren't very advisable.

44. Which would be *better?*

Being cheerful or being wise and discerning

Proverbs 17:22, 28

45. Which would be *worse?*

Being known as unfriendly or one who constantly voices foolish opinions

Proverbs 18:1-2

46. Which would be *better?*

Having good parents or a godly spouse

Proverbs 19:14

47. Which would be *better?*

Owning a lot of things or knowing a lot of things

Proverbs 20:15

48. Which would be *worse?*

Being lazy or wicked

Proverbs 21:25, 27

49. Which would be *better?*

Being blessed as a result of your generosity to the poor or being a king's best friend

Proverbs 22:9, 11

50. **Which would be *better?***

Parenting a child who grows up to be an upright, respected adult or having parents who are upright and highly respected

Proverbs 23:24-25.

51. **Which would be *worse?***

Constantly worrying about what evil people might do or being jealous of the nice things an unrighteous person owns

Proverbs 24:19

52. **Which would be *better?***

Setting an example for others with your good deeds or always doing your good deeds in secrecy

Proverbs 25:2

Which option helps you become (or remain) humbe?

53. **Which would be *better?***

Being a person who always says good things or a person who owns gold and silver

Proverbs 25:11

54. Which would be *better?*

Getting new jewelry or being rebuked by a wise person

Proverbs 25:12

55. Which would be *worse?*

A sudden snowstorm in the middle of summer or a rainstorm while you're in the middle of an outdoor project

Proverbs 26:1

56. Which would be *worse?*

Getting into an argument with a fool or being a fool

Proverbs 26:4

57. Which would be *better?*

Winning an argument with a fool or letting the fool think he's wise

Proverbs 26:5

58. Which would be *worse?*

Boasting about future prospects which never come to be or complimenting yourself in front of others

Proverbs 27:1-2

59. **Which would be *better*?**

Being tested by hard times or tested by what others have to say about you

Proverbs 27:21

60. **Which would be *better*?**

Being poor and blameless or being rich but morally worthless

Proverbs 28:6

61. **Which would be *worse*?**

Never learning from your punishments or being governed by a corrupt leader

Proverbs 29:1-2

62. **Which would be *worse*?**

Being hated because of your integrity or having an out of control temper

Proverbs 29:10-11

63. **Which would be *better*?**

Being known as someone who obeys the law or as someone who avoids making hasty, foolish comments

Proverbs 29:18-20

64. Which would be *worse?*

Being ignorant or lacking common sense

Proverbs 30:2

65. Which would be *worse?*

Lacking wisdom or lacking knowledge of God

Proverbs 30:3

66. Which would be *worse?*

Not knowing God at all or believing God exists but doubting all his words are true

Proverbs 30:4-6

67. Which would be *worse?*

Becoming extremely wealthy and deciding you don't need God or becoming extremely poor and deciding God has forgotten you

Proverbs 30:7-9

68. Which would be *better?*

Possessing the discipline of an ant or commanding the respect of a lion

Proverbs 30:25, 30

69. Which would be *worse?*

Being betrayed by an untrustworthy person or allowing alcohol to ruin your life

Proverbs 31:1-5

70. Which would be *better?*

Speaking for those who can't speak for themselves or defending those who can't defend themselves

Proverbs 31:8-9

71. Which would be *better?*

Owning a box of valuable rubies or marrying someone of noble character

Proverbs 31:10-11

72. Which would be *better?*

Having the ability to make valuable things with your hands or owning a merchant ship that travels the world

Proverbs 31:13-14

73. Which would be *better?*

Being resourceful or being shrewd

Proverbs 31:15-16

74. **Which would be *better?***

Being physically strong or giving to the poor and needy

Proverbs 31:17-20

75. **Which would be *better?***

Being wise or faithful

Proverbs 31:26